FEARLESS COMPETITORS

MMA

GAIL PARMAN

Enslow PUBLISHING

Please visit our website, www.enslow.com. For a free color catalog of all our high-quality books, call toll free 1-800-398-2504 or fax 1-877-980-4454

Published in 2027 by
Enslow Publishing
2544 Clinton Street
Buffalo, NY 14224

Portions of this work were originally authored by Peter Castellano and published as *Daredevil Sports: MMA*. All new material in this edition is authored by Gail Parman.

Cataloging-in-Publication Data
Names: Parman, Gail.
Title: MMA / Gail Parman.
Description: Buffalo, NY : Enslow Publishing, 2027. | Series: Fearless competitors | Includes glossary and index.
Identifiers: ISBN 9781978548817 (pbk.) | ISBN 9781978548824 (library bound) | ISBN 9781978548831 (ebook)
Subjects: LCSH: Mixed martial arts--Juvenile literature.
Classification: LCC GV1102.7.M59 P377 2027 | DDC 796.815 --dc23

Printed in China

Photos Credits: Cover, p. 1 Master1305/Shutterstock.com; p. 3 Ruslan Shevchenko/ Shutterstock.com; p. 3 CapturePB/Shutterstock.com; p. 3, 5, 7, 8, 10, 12, 14, 16, 18, 20, 22, 24, 26, 28 (black background) Propakages/Shutterstock.com; p. 4 Zamrznuti tonovi/Shutterstock.com; p. 6 Cassiano Correia/Shutterstock.com; p. 8 SritanaN/ Shutterstock.com; p. 10 oneinchpunch/Shutterstock.com; p. 10, 12 Wikipedia; p. 12 leolintang/Shutterstock.com; p. 14 Katherine Welles/Shutterstock.com; p. 14 Delmiro Junior/Shutterstock.com; p. 16 Kobby Dagan/Shutterstock.com; p. 18 Roka Pics/ Shutterstock.com; p. 20 gaikova/Shutterstock.com; p. 22 Tofudevil/Shutterstock.com; p. 24 Everyonephoto Studio/Shutterstock.com; p. 24 Parilov/Shutterstock.com; p. 26 Stefan Holm/Shutterstock.com; p. 29 StockphotoVideo/Shutterstock.com; p. 30 Daniil Yanopulo/ Shutterstock.com

CPSIA compliance information: Batch #QSENS27: For further information, contact Enslow Publishing, New York, New York, at 1-800-398-2504.

Contents

www.unit-sport.net
UNIT
SPORT
unit-sport.net
unit
unit

FIGHTERS READY!

Two MMA fighters face off. They circle the fighting area, daring one another to throw a punch. Finally, one does. His **opponent** ducks and tries a kick. Each fighter grabs the other, and one is pushed to the ground. The crowd around them roars with a loud cheer.

FEARLESS FACTS

MMA fighting can be dangerous. All MMA fighting and training should be done with the help of a good coach. Don't try these moves on your own!

UFC
Reebok

MIXING STYLES

MMA is a sport that mixes many styles of martial arts from around the world. It stands for "mixed martial arts." MMA fighters have training in several different **disciplines**, such as boxing, wrestling, judo, karate, and more. Because they come from different martial arts backgrounds, fighters each have their own **style**.

FEARLESS FACTS

Both men and women **compete** in MMA, though not against each other. They fight in separate **divisions**.

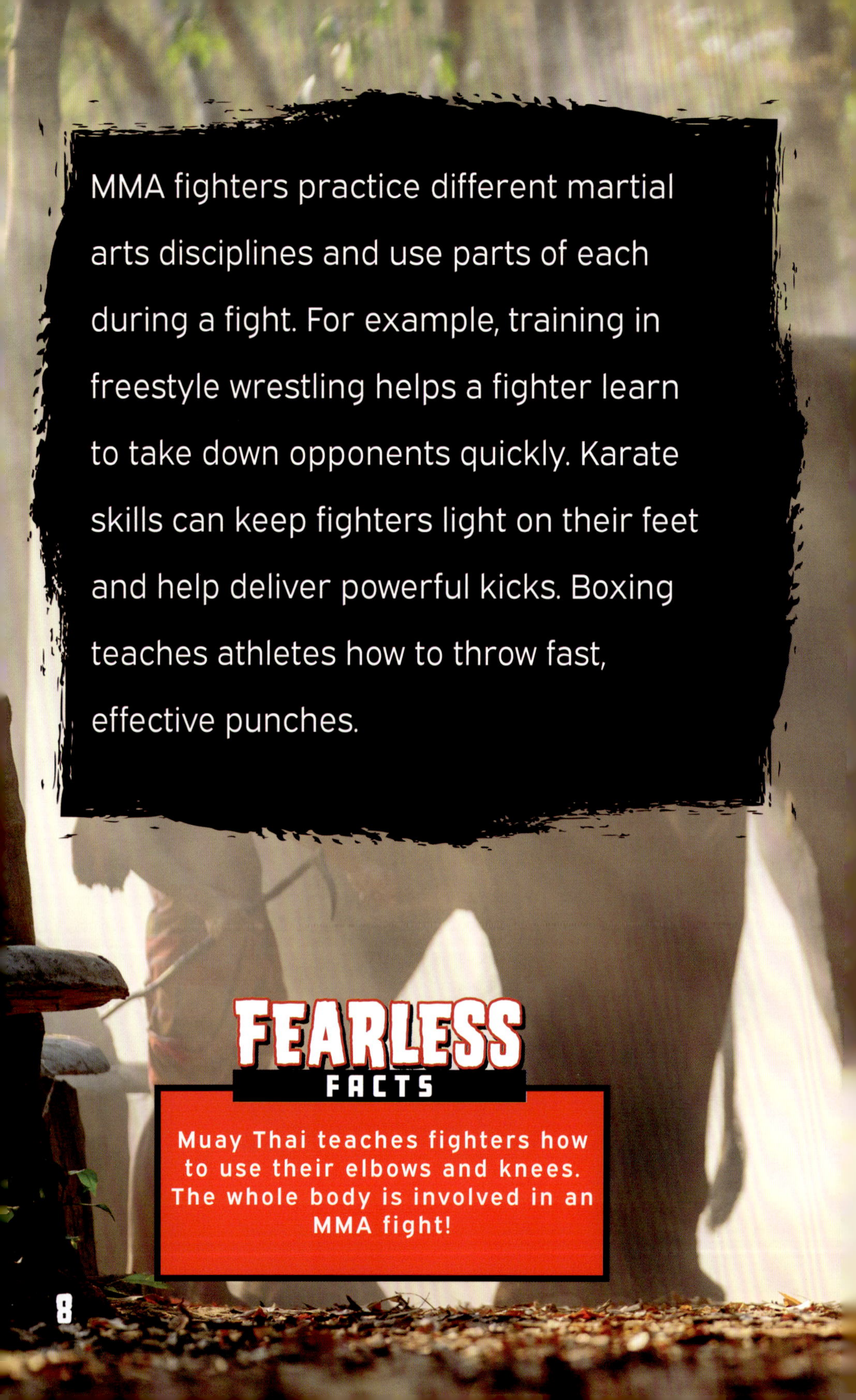

MMA fighters practice different martial arts disciplines and use parts of each during a fight. For example, training in freestyle wrestling helps a fighter learn to take down opponents quickly. Karate skills can keep fighters light on their feet and help deliver powerful kicks. Boxing teaches athletes how to throw fast, effective punches.

FEARLESS FACTS

Muay Thai teaches fighters how to use their elbows and knees. The whole body is involved in an MMA fight!

THE HISTORY OF MMA

MMA as we know it today began in 1993. But the idea of mixing fighting styles started much earlier. In the late 1800s, Asian martial artists and European fighters sometimes competed. In 1967, actor and martial artist Bruce Lee created jeet kune do. Some call him the first modern mixed martial artist.

FEARLESS FACTS

Jeet kune do is a fighting style that pulls from the disciplines of wing chun, tai chi, tae kwon do, boxing, fencing, and jiu-jitsu.

FEARLESS FACTS

The fight between Ali and Inoki is often seen as a step toward the beginning of modern MMA.

MMA BEGINS

In 1993, the Ultimate Fighting Championship (UFC) began. A group of martial artists and fighters wanted to see how each fighting discipline compared, so they put the best fighters against one another. From this first UFC event, modern MMA fighting was born.

FEARLESS FACTS

The UFC is the best-known MMA organization. It holds events around the world and has gained a huge following of fans.

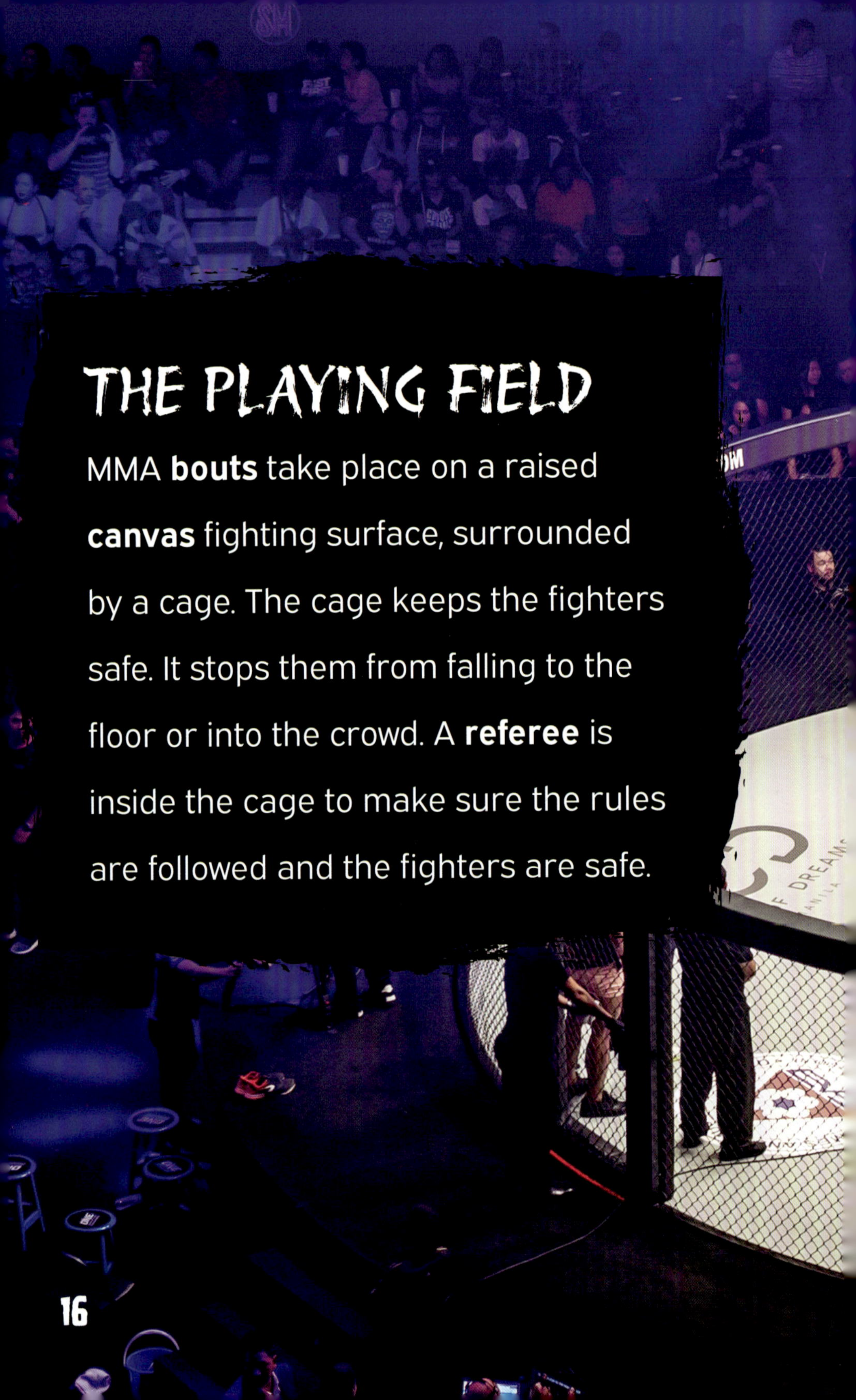

THE PLAYING FIELD

MMA **bouts** take place on a raised **canvas** fighting surface, surrounded by a cage. The cage keeps the fighters safe. It stops them from falling to the floor or into the crowd. A **referee** is inside the cage to make sure the rules are followed and the fighters are safe.

FEARLESS FACTS

MMA is also known as "cage fighting" because of the sport's fighting area. In the UFC, the cage is called the "octagon" because it has eight sides.

During an MMA competition, there are several bouts lasting three rounds each. Rounds are five minutes long, with a one-minute break in between. Fighters hit each other with punches, elbows, and knees. They may push one another into the cage or to the ground.

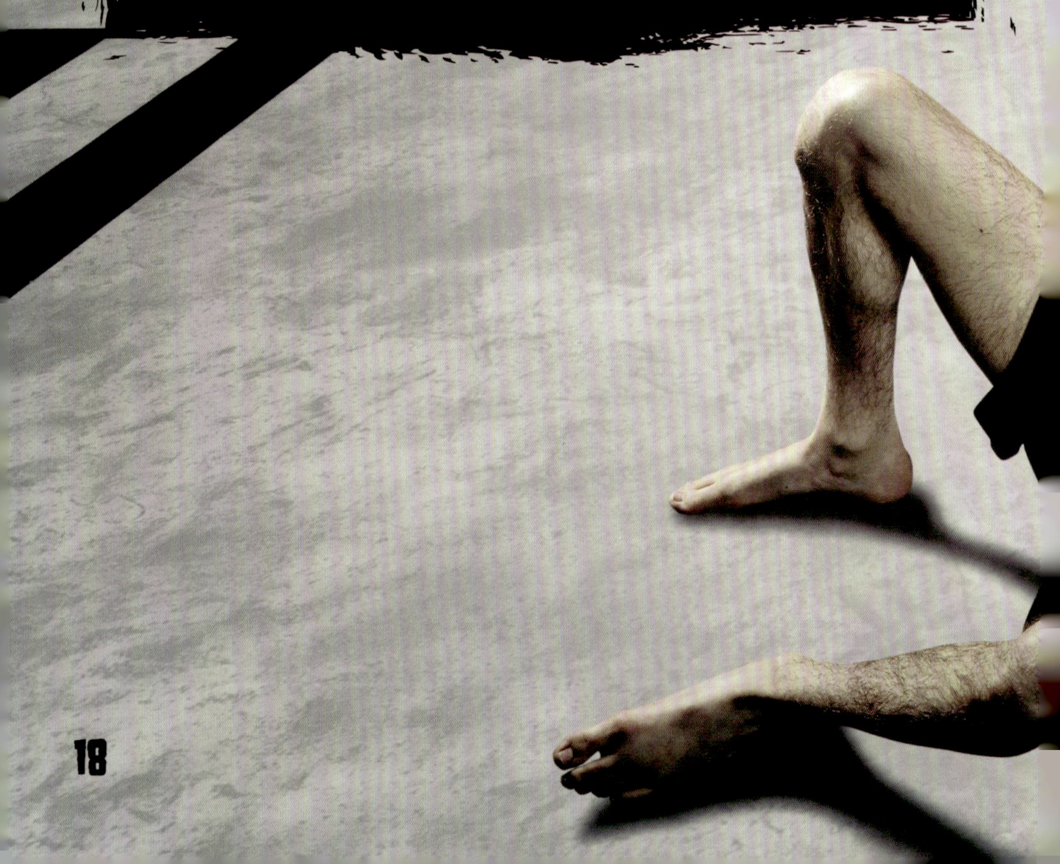

FEARLESS FACTS

Fighters can win if their opponent is unable to continue, if their opponent **concedes**, or if the judges declare one fighter as the winner.

SCORING POINTS

During each bout, three judges sit on different sides of the cage. They watch the fighters carefully and give each one a score to decide who wins each round. Points can be earned by effective kicks and punches, taking down opponents, and controlling the fighting area.

FEARLESS FACTS

An MMA fight can end with the judges choosing the winner based on the points each fighter earned. When the judges' points determine the winner, it's called winning by "decision."

DECLARING A WINNER

Sometimes MMA fights end in a knockout (KO). This happens when one fighter is hit too hard or injured and cannot continue. In a technical knockout (TKO), a referee or doctor announces the winner. A TKO is called when continuing the fight seems unsafe for one of the fighters.

FEARLESS FACTS

A fight can also end by "submission," when one fighter has trapped their opponent in a certain hold. The trapped fighter shows they've given up by tapping the mat or the other fighter. This is called "tapping out."

FOLLOW THE RULES

MMA can be a dangerous sport, so rules are created to keep fighters as safe as possible. Today, most MMA competitions use a set of rules that state the size of the cage, give directions about judging, and even tell fighters how to wrap their hands.

FEARLESS FACTS

When the UFC started, MMA had few rules. It was often criticized for being unsafe and violent.

MMA fighters lose points if they break the rules. They can even be disqualified, or taken out of the bout, for breaking too many of them. There's no biting, hair pulling, grabbing of the throat, or kneeing the head of an opponent on the ground.

FEARLESS FACTS

Fighters may kick, throw, and punch their opponents during bouts—but they don't want to injure them too much. Sportsmanship is important!

A FAIR FIGHT

Today, weight classes make sports like MMA fairer. All fighters must be weighed to make sure they're fighting someone close to their own size. The weight classes in MMA include featherweight, lightweight, heavyweight, and more. Fighters have to weigh in before each bout.

FEARLESS FACTS

Today, there are 11 weight classes, ranging from athletes weighing 105 pounds (47.6 kg) to those weighing up to 265 pounds (120 kg).

VENUM

Safety First

ALL MMA FIGHTERS SHOULD:

- follow the rules when fighting an opponent.
- never compete injured.
- not compete too often, so their body can recover between bouts.
- stay fit in other ways. It will help them hold up during bouts and recover more easily.
- know how to keep themselves safe in the cage.

For More Information

BOOKS

Kortemeier, Todd. *Superstars of the UFC.* Amicus Ink, 2017.

Shapiro, Sean. *Mixed Martial Arts Strategies.* Abdo Publishing, 2024.

Terp, Gail. *MMA.* Black Rabbit Books, 2025.

WEBSITES

MMA Fighting

www.mmafighting.com

Read about the latest events and some of the best fighters competing today.

7 Types of MMA Fighting Styles

www.themadlabmma.com/mma-fighting-styles/

Find out more about the blend of fighting styles used in MMA.

Publisher's note to educators and parents: Our editors have carefully reviewed these websites to ensure that they are suitable for students. Many websites change frequently, however, and we cannot guarantee that a site's future contents will continue to meet our high standards of quality and educational value. Be advised that students should be closely supervised whenever they access the Internet.

Glossary

bout: an athletic match

canvas: a strong cloth

compete: to try to win in a contest

concede: to give up

discipline: a kind of training

divisions: groups of athletes with similar characteristics

opponent: the person or team you must beat to win a game

referee: an official who makes sure players follow the rules

style: a certain way of doing something

Index